SEEING IT WAS SO

SEEING IT WAS SO

POEMS BY

ANTHONY PICCIONE

BOA EDITIONS, LTD. · BROCKPORT, NEW YORK · 1986

Grateful acknowledgment is made to the editors of journals and publishers of chapbooks in which some of the poems in this book first appeared: *The Brockport Forum, Choice, The Iowa Review, Loblolly*; Banjo Press, Mammoth Press, Rook Press and Serviceberry Press.

To Al, Barry, Bill, Bob, Dan, Gary, Jeff, Jo, Leslie, Lucien and Tony: Thanks, friends! Special thanks to Michael Waters who has helped so greatly, from the beginning.

—A.P.

ISBN: 0-918526-50-7 Cloth; 0-918526-51-5 Paper.

Publications by BOA Editions, Ltd., a not-for-profit corporation under section 501(c)(3) of the United States Internal Revenue Service Code, are made possible in part with the assistance of grants from the Literature Program of the New York State Council on the Arts and the Literature Program of the National Endowment for the Arts, a Federal Agency.

BOA logo by Mirko.
Cover drawing of Han-shan from a Japanese woodblock print of a Chinese rubbing.
Designed and typeset at Visual Studies Workshop, Rochester, N.Y.

Distributed by Bookslinger, 213 E. Fourth Street, St. Paul, Minnesota 55101.

First Edition

BOA Editions, Ltd.
A. Poulin, Jr., President
92 Park Avenue
Brockport, N.Y. 14420

My father, my mother,
Ginny the rejoicer,
Lisa, Rachel, Sarah, and Todd,
our wild-hearted children,
for them

and with homage to
the mad Chinese saints

CONTENTS

THE SKY

DISCOVERING THE SKY AT SIX YEARS

My slow and only friend points first.
We run all morning, the smoking fields and trees
part once more, once more.
I stop dumb at the last easy hill,
then, rushing to touch it, it rushes away.
It's farther than I thought, I think.
Waited too damn long, my friend says.

WITH MY COUSIN MITCH, NIGHT OF THE QUARTER MOON, I PLACE A TURD IN THE SOAPDISH AND GO IN TO SHOW THE GROWNUPS

It is riverbed-yellow, flecked with mica,
a secret so vast and simple, it is the turnback
of a million years that fills us with wonder.

It fits, precisely, the soapdish's curve.
How can this be? We walk in slowly, unfold
this oracle. My mother loves the joke, the holiness

perhaps, while his lifts a thin switch of ash,
the grim lines of her face already twitching.
There is something we don't understand here,

it was my idea, my lost way that got us to this place.
And how can a pinch of clay scatter so many so far?

AUGUST 1944, LEAVING A BIBLE CLASS
AT SUNDAY SCHOOL

Out in the air that settles lightly
over Old Testament figs you suddenly inhale,
the rough table rimmed with guests, the holy man
in the bare yard, eyes so fiercely set

they find the boy's stare burning above
a page of Jerusalem. When
I walk slowly home without shoes,
the feet of the brain rising and sinking

across all summer at a grandmother's grave,
her softness her name, the flower smell
of the thought, the world lodged so deeply in the body,

the part of us that is bird
begins to scatter and look down as I pass
the small cemetery called Creek Stand.

Thirty centuries of sky blaze at midday,
the bright robes of the watchful
floating over my breathing

and this boy, this solitude that turns
the page to find us again in the long
wake of our stumbling joyful lives.

FIRST COMMUNION

If it is night here I will wake in Jerusalem shivering.
Far below, an ant pushes a dungball
up the cobble hill to my feet, so I lift my rifle
and send tiny black stars into the soldiers' foreheads.
Jesus, his poor ruined face, looks up, amazed, down.
A hot wind lifts our breath blazing through his crown
as thorns, bone chips of antlers fly off around us.

Now the crowd sways and falls back down the path.
Our brother, the soft fish body alive and alone,
starts calmly through the streets. Empty and dim, there
is no end, I know, to this dream. Jesus, this circle
is tighter even as it lightens and shrinks. Listen,
everyone sweet and cruel, we die or rise, amazed.

BEING LAZY IN A FIELD OF WILD RYE

So many seeds. How young boys love women! These stems have been bare for centuries. Entire populations wave from the tips. The old desire is real. Dreams, hairs drift in the air at midday.

The long root in the stag's underbelly points to the sky.

FATHER KLARMAN, SAINT MARGARET'S
ROMAN CATHOLIC CHURCH

You turned away just as you spoke the truth,
the sneer in the corner of your smile,
your indignant eyes dull before God the Storm
you told of, my own storm lessening,
the first few feet of drift so vast, my way
already lost as the light left anywhere I stepped.

Now these twenty years of night,
fear boiling in the brain, stripped, dumb,
grace a condition of thought to be fought for,
the old joy so dim it was true —
Father, confess and save us both.

In this morning's dream something soft whispered
through the keyhole with a faint hiss. Margaret,
Saint of children, see to him first.

BOY IN THE DARK

This is the summer I hide under five blankets,
smothering, as we watch the camp gates scream
open, the dead stacked like words in the newsreels.

This is the sleep that sends lost bodies
burning across night, the tongue bitten off,
forgiveness choked in the throat.

This is the room we wake to, the walls
strung with shadow, windows shattered with light.
In his uniform, the keeper stares wildly at his own children.

THE ANGELS OF RESURRECTION

Start in the beginning then. Breathe,
push the crushed frond back out
to the sun, wake the first snail,
the veins in the frog's throat.

Nothing has failed. When you call us
we can lie down here too.

FROM THE BIRTH THREADS

Musk, and river reeds scraping,
I cry river-mad, the breath like a pulse

already measuring things. I look
down, feet wild and lifting free.

Where to stop, step?

Across the blood's hum,

the names of my daughters,
the small wind shaking on shore

where night softens and turns
and settles for now for sleep.

AND IF

Adrift on a float in a pool, nothing to do.
Birds draw near, unafraid.
And sometimes, right now, the blank sky
crimps down and claims all you've named.

No matter. That part with no memory can't rest either.
Its lines are out, tangling past shore, through smoke,
the mind with a thousand grappling hooks to the future.

Something must give. Wave fear aside.
Move. Embrace friends. Swim a little.

I'D END UP

In awe in aloneness
talking as though to God

in the words that fall ahead
through the snowbank cloud

in all that is left undone
between the call and silence

this is where I'd end up stumbling
in the homecoming anywhere

OUTSIDE, NAKED

It is dawn and I have not slept,
this joy is so complete.

Crickets wake in my ears,
feet freezing in the wet grass.

I know, grinning, that only
a fool forgets his shoes.

LATE MORNING POEM

All night the universe fell and falls headfirst
through the ache of black and pinpoint
light, the mind thinning farther, yet farther.

Awake. The sun returns. I am a man.
Still, this dream could stretch out and touch
beginning and end, tonight maybe.

SITTING UP IN BED

SHORTEST DAY OF THE YEAR,
EVERYTHING SAYS YES

Open my eyes, for today you must be closest.
Well, we die at this tree,
we die and still we know nothing.

My child's tiny flame strains to light
all there is that you have made. The wise turn
from us with a half-smile that eats my cheek.

I am tired talking through this wall,
oh Lord of breath, my bones are cold
my head snaps back before I can speak.

Torn out of women and now
no place to rest, this great homelessness,
there is something familiar to it.

And you are gone even as the will awakes.
Our backs are frozen to your wall,
oh Giver of everything. We cannot move.

The path is covered with names, the word sifted
and split through thousands of mouths. Those
exiles freezing in darkness, were they not bravest?

Still, we feel everywhere for you, beyond the edge
and emptiness that lifts and crashes
over the first thought in any direction.

Are we here to be crazy? What can we give?
This starving in the brain, is it mine?
Say *go* or *stay*, oh Storm of minds.

We are yet here, our lips move before the sound,
the man-books have begun again to close, those who can live
hug the gift. And these questions? Lord, we think to love you.

TURNING TO FACE THE POEM

Hanging old worksocks out to dry
on the back fence, asking nothing,

I am filled with such laziness
that I love everything at once.

I don't know, I don't know,
even joy has death in it.

The black sonic boom. All day
the eyes blink black, light.

This fear is no friend. When
you stand up, it falls aside.

SATURDAY AT THE CABIN

Haul the white kitchen table from the 1920s,
set it in south window, grinning and lazy.
Read Snyder, eat lunch, chest and belly full.
Spel Against Demons takes that guy and washes
him and warns him one more time. Sun down.
Night surrounds and squeezes under the door.

Up to ankles in dark voices, shout-words
like *CHINA* and *CHILE* and *UGANDA*. Let fall
the calm poem of light, it curls and shrinks
and is swallowed. What is this? Scramble
onto tabletop, both boots lost to a suckhole.
Nightsticks bob and nod *yes*. Low sigh like *Chicago*.

Television silent all month. Thank God no news.
Eat my heart anyway. Last year's *Newsweek*
moaning in my hands. What's this? Death smoke
trapped and aching for heaven in my starlit head.
I call out, the sin-eater alone on the table.

A knife raises itself in the east as people
see each other for the first time. Stab-pains
in our chests. Lie down with these poor bastards.
No one leaves this place, not yet. Steer our boat
towards shore. Get down, walk home for supper.
Pray out loud. I don't know. Wash my bloody hands.

AT A COLD BEACH

Two people gather sticks
for the small fire that may not last.
It rages like a child at their feet.

All night she has tasted emptiness
and now rushes to fill his cup with wine.
He has flung his weapons into the sea.

Drunk, the man stares at the waves.
They love each other, the fire, the shore.

TRAVELLING COMPANION

I am so tired I can lie down here
in the long shadow-hair of rocks even as
the old two-edged voice begins to worry.

Words boil and pull and leave their losses,
questions that track down hope, that sleep with insects,
that chew in my sleep the lives of small things.

It is no use. Get up. Shake the ants
out of my shirt. And at my feet
and in daylight, the cold brother who will not speak.

NOW A FEW SILENCES

Another night and we are soon free of gifts.
The quiet one is sleepy and fluffs her pillow just so,
I set out for the next world inside my colorless thirst
and this is close to love and here is our century.
We are like friends gone still on death night.
We twist our hands and say *see, see*, it was true.

CAMOUFLAGE

The feverish priest in his sweet black gown
glows like a woman who has stepped from the sea.

The swamp lies awake. The worm-shaped tongue shivers
with slow fishing in the mouth and slime of the snapping turtle.

Just now, crosstown, a heavy woman glowers at subway toughs
and the man next door says *yes, all right,* to a towering love.

June outside. Mindless fireflies stir in sleepy lust.
The saw-jawed beetle also waves his twin lantern light.

Yes, and in these nights of thick wine and thoughts of salvation
I finger the times I hurt my lover. The fists on my desk are loaves.

ICE FISHING

I stand two days staring
into the black hole.
The slowness fills
with seawater. Ice mountains
blaze all around.
Every thing's mind sweeps over me.
We meet our own eyes.

INSIDE THE GREAT DOUBT

That bright shape that has swum
spinning all week through the brain
now turns and crashes out
into the light of its own awakening.

Each shivering piece of my life
hurtles in and out again, the long
thoughts lasting a second longer
before the blinding face I cannot see.

Survivors gather half-fearfully nearby.
The family, beggars, animals, the child
at dawn—who knows what this day means
except that it has come with no past?

I know I am dying outside on a lawn.
I somersault my goodbye at the edge.
Thoughts of death bunch at last
inside one soft, huffing of breath

over the dark length of the universe.
The star-packed form sits up,
blesses and banishes me,
and lies slowly back down.

I dive all night towards earth,
fully lost and closer to home.

NEXT WE LEAVE OUR CHILDREN
IN THE NEW WORLD

1

I'll stare at her and survive, I think,
the chest suddenly free of feeling.
We'll sit stunned in our dreamy kitchen.
I'll need my things, follow the few
back down the mantrails away from streets.

2

Then she turns from the black stove,
her fingernails smoking with terror.
Dust is drifting inside sunlight.
The father studies his own hands.
This takes thirty thousand years.

3

I have cast my life at the edge just to see.
My children grow far. We know the world
has left us this time. I'll do what I can.
I will not look down again except to die.

SONG TO MY CHILDREN

But then I dreamed I wouldn't go down and wouldn't, except that
I rose amazed and waking at the praying wall just as my luck
struck me from behind and my back to the wall for sure this time.

I spit on that song. Your faces crinkle with light.
Ah, and now when I put my slow round shoulder to it,
the great dull Buddha bell in the tower unbudging,
see, it moves, just once, the first faint ONG struck
from nothing, away, back, the space-buoy in the chest,
the black all-sound swelling everywhere, the puffy heart
lost at last and my name lies down in the dark to die.
Yes, and even in this we find ourselves sick unto death.
Forty years I cried out. Soon the bright one must surely wake.

SITTING UP IN BED

Something cold has thrown me from sleep.
Upstairs, the children drift on their sides of stars.

I know this vigil, I'll stare at the dark,
night may weaken and drop all its stones.

Death still weaves a shawl for my shoulders.
It is soft and so I draw it closer.

Sunrise. At last the birds can take their shapes.
Now a man whistles, feeling for shoes with his feet.

FOR THE LOST KINGDOM

A TOAST TO MY BIRTHDAY

This head is too small for such craving,
that is why I love what cannot be held.
My cup empties itself over the dark yard.
Adrift, lost up to the throat in red wine,
I invite my sins to cast themselves free.
When I raise this drink and look down,
the grass stares, weeps into my feet.

SHIRALI MISLIMOV, WORLD'S OLDEST MAN

So, I get up early in the morning,
work naked in my garden
and go to bed just after ten in the evening.

Of my 23 children, two are alive,
the rest were carried away by storms.
I thought my bones were burning
so I drank whiskey. That was 1851.

My wife is full of power
and looks steadily at me.
I say never sleep in the daytime.

DRINKING WITH MY FATHER ON MY BIRTHDAY

We won't speak for years.
But I have climbed again at dawn
to the top of this mad Long Island
pine above his hidden yard.
I am happy and drink
red wine from a gallon.

He slumps there, a rack of forty coats
getting drunk with silent guests.
He raises his empty glass to the sky,
something red burns through his eyes
and makes him cough and look down.

I fill my chest with hot wine
and lean away for another year.

HAVING LUNCH WITH A FAMOUS POET

We walk in his wife's rose garden,
his arm incredibly around me.
The pace grows wrong, his cold hand
burns through sweaters to my shoulder,
a kind of envy stiffens between us.
What are we afraid of?
Words cling to our shoes and moan.

IN A GORGE WITH A FRIEND

We sit up all night by a lantern
at the bottom talking about God.
The light gives itself to the dark

in all directions. The soft
cut of the sides swallows our words
in kindness. We're still a little jumpy,
animal shapes draw near and disappear.

Drinking whiskey like this, we love each
other, we know we're a million
years down. And the climb can wait.

PRAYER IN ALL DIRECTIONS

Dig my feet in the pink weeds of sunset.
Night, lose this place skyward, head out
into the black spattered with faint lights.

This morning, returned, one sweet and sloughing hand
wakes on the slopes of my hairy neck.
Looking for home, even the sleeper is called.

SATURDAY, ORANG CHILDREN HUG MY LEGS

The day is filled with light
and my children play in high joy.
Adrift near the edge, I see
the hairy red arms hurl a stick
like a toy, the bright blackness
then curl over it like lips.

There are days like this.
In the smallest way
we are known to ourselves.

BURYING THE BARN SWALLOW

It was a long week pried loose
from the jaws of our cat,
and now this, though

our children show us how.
We place a sunflower seed under
the pale tongue and plant her, head up.

We walk home together, nearly free.
There is the summer before us,
we can wait for the song to grow.

TODAY

You walk around thinking, at last
the earth, my God, means me,
the breath half given, the mouth of loose teeth,
the bone-ache of all stems is in it too.
Hope grows calmer. Our feet
rise and fall with simple ease.

NEW POLITICS

1

Who knows what hand this is
that claps a man
in the back of the head
and makes him leave the ground
every third step like an oaf!

2

And when was it we were led away to work for the dead?
Today I called in sick and happy
and joined the movement to make Wednesday
the tiny work-week for screw-offs,
the violinist with a phone tucked
under her chin as she cooks,
the father who loves singing and clatter at the table,
the farmer whose tractor is a raft on the river,
the factory worker who starts busily about
when the boss glides in,
and anyone else who is born to playfulness.

3

Today even the President stayed home,
blushing, the long oath of brotherhood
written on the inside of his sleeve.
Stand him up where we can see him,
on television, like an expensive prize.
Soon the land will wake with a clear head.

WATCHING THE SUN SINK

This day has fallen from me too,
just out of reach, like a town
below the horizon you can almost see.

I have been happy thinking like this,
lying down near the names of things.

Now the low pond is busy.
Tonight it is an older woman's desire—
she still loves us deeply, halfway to the other world.

LYING DOWN BY THE POND

The long afternoon, gray light
pondering gray light. At last
the muddy spatter, small throat uplifted,
a sputtering of feathers. Drifting.
Listen, brother, you may live forever!

Sweet madness so close
that I do not move. This is his bath.
Oh Lord of faces, what is it
that fills us? What is sparrow?

JULY 3, 1949

Then it was my tenth birthday and I grew happy,
thinking wide about the Chinese egg in *Ripley*'s.
In early morning, the world just waking,
I placed my egg and letter in a jam jar
in a hole by the drainpipe's oak sapling
and turned toward the dim face a hundred
years ahead. Across the crash of traffic and nightmare
tangle I prayed for those words buried in simple hope
and the sky rose up and held true all summer.

WAKING IN PEKING

I rise staring at my empty overcoat.
My shoes wait, filling with dim light.

Outside, in air of bread, in sweat of work,
a bicycle with its sidecar slides by.
The child waves his cap. Noise takes the street.

A stiff wind holds under my own breathing.
Here. I touch my chest. I am yet here,
fool of my forty-third year. This pleases

me, this loss and gain, this wide sprawling search
opening onto dream, this strangeness, this earth.

WITH WHITMAN AT THE FRIENDSHIP HOTEL

I call out crazed in fever in a room
in Peking where I've come afraid and alone
to find, something, the words maybe.
My family looks out from the gulf behind
their photographs on the rickety desk.

So I stand. With a bottle of red wine
and no talk for days, no talk
from my neighbors puzzled and rushed,
the Chinese frozen in awe untouching,
and here, in the chest of all that is lost,
I read, out loud, Walt Whitman.

Someone's voice cracks, gathers, grows
calm by my feet on the green wash of rug,
and waves this meeting aside. Brother,
brother, here is our home. Who knows
what powers the world! I love the man.

EIGHT A.M., FROM A THIRD FLOOR BALCONY
(Friendship Hotel, Peking)

Now the companion is shoved awake,
bored, feeling a little crazy today.
Let's get out of bed and stand naked.
Let's walk around and around in our sandals.
You put things in place just so—
hang the toothbrush on a string
over the tub away from bugs.
I'll stare and survey my narrow kingdom.

The small shapes of women moving
the treasure upstream, such soft distance—
like the gulf between me this morning
and my wild sleeping animal flesh,
like the continent between both of us
and, say, sin, here, faintly in the mouth,
like the tiny sour footprints of the roach
out onto the tightwire to my toothbrush.

CHRISTMAS EVE, PEKING

A few lights, a voice or two lifted along
these glint-gray streets gone empty with
people bent towards their own belonging.

The breast aches out over the earth's
curve: wife, daughters, homeland
safe somehow in their gathering dawn.

I will spend this night looking
into the face of forgiveness,
the dark Chinese heads turning.

FOR THE LOST KINGDOM:
THIS POEM WITH NO SOLDIERS IN IT

Two archways mirror each other in marble,
dragon-lions glare at the frozen sky, waiting,
the Emperor of earth, air and oceans, gone.

I look for the small stones of dynasty.
The woman gathers a bouquet of brown weeds,
a kind of love across such distance, waving.

Together now in simple nearness, we study each
other. There is French wine. Her face burns.
We know this place. We do not touch and do not touch.

NAPPING OUTSIDE

ATOMS

How we fall all night towards each other,
the speed of longing gathered in our far flung hearts.

TRYING TO READ IN MY STUDY

Buddha, St. Theresa, Lao Tsu, the dancing
bears in the window backed with storm.
A blackbird crosses left to right.
The empty window brighter.

WHILE LEANING OVER TO SAY SOMETHING

Something moving around down there,
rubbings and yawns in the back of the head.
The invisible keeps speaking, our faces stay blank.

I'm mad? Look at me! Straighten my tie!

EXCHANGE

Who knows where thought ends and spirit begins?
Our dog licks my feet of salt!

GARDENING

An early morning happiness
swarms through my chest—
even toes forget their moorings.

TO MY NEIGHBOR IN BLOSSOMING SLEEP

If it is true that seeds of stars
stir yawning in the soft veins,
then tell me, who are we,
and when shall we wake?

PILGRIMS STANDING AROUND AT MID-POINT

What is it but a slowness grown fond
of the path, a sudden joyful sloth
between here and death, like, say,
grinning in the dark with one eye open!

LOOKING AT STARS AND FALLING OUTWARD

We disappear into everything.
Atoms shudder and stir,
rock begins to speak its silence.
All is said, even our names.

LOVE POEM

We touch each other.
The eternal
fans the planet
egg awake.

AFTER LOVE

When the great net lowers itself over even
lives like ours, and we fall forward like this,
the tiny spark of longing lighting the way,
then, listen, what have we to do with less?

AT THE LAKE SHORE

Neighbors wave shyly, we know what we're here for.
The lake stuns our feet, washes them.

NAPPING OUTSIDE

It is the last of summer.
Light hums between the sunflowers
and our frog pond.
What did we dream of?

GOING NORTH

FIRST NIGHT, FOR MY FAMILY

It is a one-man cabin where things
almost fit. So I drink wine alone and
grinning, my children safe and far in their photographs.

I keep putting small things in place and think
hard about the black ant tribe along the wall.
Finally I poison only my shoes and the legs of the cot.

How restless this life is without women.
And where did I find my longing for night,
its thin breath rising and falling around me?

Look. Because I love you fifty miles to the north,
I can lie down in still darkness
and disappear, with my arms open.

THE BACK FIELD

It is a small fire and I have lain too near
for hours. Still, I do not move. My back fits
the cold back-shaped dusk of early spring.
I am so alone this time that even my sorrow
draws away. Constellations of the first few lights,
I see they are shaggy plants. Their faint kinship
lifts me to my frog dream where the warm stems
of everything drift sideways.
Blue star stems waver into place.

Now the hoot owl lowers her voice once, twice.
My dog returns from his solitary life,
the roots of the world snuffed up into
his tiny child's brain packed with happiness.
Night. Christ, I will not move until called.

NIGHT CAMPING

I have stared for two days, not speaking.
Trees. Pine, oak, maple, the family that stands.

A storm arrives and I hug myself closer.
What is it that I climbed forty years for and lost?

Late night, a weak fire. I feel good beneath
the black drift of sky, slow in the cold air,
and lift my face to the rain as once long ago.

AT THE CABIN, NOVEMBER MOVING

A little rain, so the pond is up
over the frogs' freezing sleep.
The few trees stand calmly in the grass,
only I am restless and walk
the small shore.
                 Two Canada geese
wait tensing in the watery brush for my going,
a family. The dark eyes of the female
hurry over me and look down. God,
I say to her. Nothing moves, except a wind
that hurls and trills about the bone
white cold from beyond. I want to go home.

OUTSIDE

After the first sleet snow the talking goes silent.
Inside my long walk, testing the cold in clumsy stiffness,
field and woods drifting over, away into the bone length of it,
the weather we can't, alive, reach, I measure, measure, lose.

Autumn lingers like a room, a face we glimpsed as we locked
our greenhouse against winter. And for the deermouse, trapped
or lodged by choice, we stumble back again and again
to set out cracked corn and a tent of shirts.

Still, an awkward distance presses tight
behind my walking, windows iced and growing faint,
head leaning into the shearing wind, time and
place a small light around my feet.

WINTER, LOOKING FOR SURVIVORS

We waited and slept, felt the far lights
of farmhouses slam out and go aground, wind
taking more than breath, the human swagger
flattened, pressed so small our ways crowd
and tower like lies, the skyline gone overnight
and how to rise? Do we know ourselves or not?

It was a winter, we will say, that dropped people
like rags, showed us touch that left our shoulders
white. Our backs grew long hair, the planet at last
teaching—neighbors, do we look alike or not?
Along the frozen bud-shoot too silent this time,
down to the stunned dream roots, or not?

A lost white hand goes up, barely a wave.
I would give my own hairy life for less.

OPENING THE CABIN AT MID-WINTER

Now, this is really splendid, a gift!
The mad scrawl of mouse dung over my desk,
dark tunneling through the ruins of mattress,
dumb scrabbling feet gone still in the walls,
all of this where nothing was! Joy balanced
on a hair, bright sky unfolding, and rage.

VISIT FROM A FRIEND

Spring flood again. Went out to not write the poem,
to not find my name under the uprooted poplar,
to see my white feet as just mine, two small
lazy things to be loved one at a time.

His car pulls in. Too fast. Still, I dream with animals.
So hard to know what century this is. Sitting here,
like this, cities lean in around the brickmaker.
Legs numb for years. Shift. Move.

While my tall friend points rightly to books and men,
we watch a hummingbird surround the slow mind of the sky.
Soon the only thing moving, we know, is what we think.
Now the whole history of libraries blazes like a match.

If this is not the world, why are we here?
Well, we will call this silence the universe
where our children find their play in all directions,
and this time forgive them us, if it goes that way.

TWO POEMS AFTER WINTER

A SMALL PRAYER TO EVERYTHING

Is there somewhere we shouldn't look? What wins with a trick?
To the dark Mothers, and the Fathers of outrage,
and anything powerful that calls for my heart, take it.
It happens that I am finished with fear. I don't know why
I got here, nor what it means to dive all night towards God,
but I'm awake now, beside this slow buffalo who chews
even the sunlight as it falls on the grass.
Well, I am going to lie down here, for nothing.
Love to you, to the brain we share: it holds only where we go.

THIS DAY OF SPRING, WE ALL GO OUTSIDE

Kneeling in the high grass, patching a fence, at last
I climb down from that spindly mind that held the skies
of winter off, losing, losing. Now the whole world
is busy. Our dog plunges everywhere with no name.
The two little ones play and play. My wife lies
down naked in the back fields of sun, it's our land.
Her breasts are so white, so utterly soft, so free
of meaning I go over just to be near. I love this laziness.
Today, I know, I will worry no more weeds from the word-brain,
today, I tell her, I give myself to the buffalo.
We laugh and shove each other. Totally happy,
our teenage daughter rides past on the small yellow tractor.

THIS WORLD IS ANYTHING ALL AT ONCE

Tonight, over wine, my inside
says softly, as though to no one,
the notes in a bird are fixed and eternal.
A crisp stillness powers the room

until I walk out over the startled fields
to stand upright with trees in the cold.
The pond glows. Stars, and the low fire of fish eggs.

I think of my daughters who breathe without trying,
my wife by the flowerbed that gives only flowers.

Tonight, oh trillion-throated one, I love you
in all of your songs, especially women.

FOR LOVE, FOR MY WIFE

Blackness with no edge or thought
but now a slow dim petal
of delicate touch or the light
hand cupped over your sex
and, ah, your love has called you
to sweet fire up from nowhere except
night which must be the soul asleep
it is so vast and so complete.

SEEING BEHIND ME

The small creek boils with brown muscle into my pond. Twelve, my friend counts. Lake bass, big as legs, circle and circle. We stand on the cabin roof drinking wine. As many times as we count, they are twelve. We look up, down, drink more wine. Something like soft power seizes my head and squeezes all I can see backwards, that boy in July glimpsing God's bright feet in the back of the church, joy in the chest lifting us an inch or two towards ourselves. Why twelve? Why men, or fish?

ASYLUM

Take me, you want to say even as you are taken.
Here is the night when darkness swallows itself

and we climb back down starless and freezing
from nobody's century

and the names of the lost
are washed hungry and safe onto shore

and the mad father who squints at the sky
and then at his watch is led to the table

and what is born holds a small light
fanned up from women

and we love the wet shivering heart
that knows it cannot leave this place.

Now doorways are seen to be doorways,
the house filling at last with joyful people.

WHAT DO YOU WANT WHEN YOU LEAVE?

Delirium in the touch of women,
that softness, I think.

Flesh to the tongue of melon,
of nations inside the grainseed,
of the sweet curve over bread.
Flesh on the lives of our children.

But what do you leave when you leave?

That rising up from sleep in the brainstem,
I think, that softness without touch.

GOING NORTH

A hundred miles north of the treeline
the last renegade tree.
Sit down. Sit down.

Soon you hear above the howling
the voice forgiving everything.
Lie down.

A simple plant
out of the top of the forehead,
just a spruce.

Birds nest there
though it's not theirs either.
Be still.

ANTHONY PICCIONE

Anthony Piccione was born in Sheffield, Alabama, in 1939. He graduated from East Texas State University, the University of Texas–El Paso, where he studied poetry with Robert Burlingame, and Ohio University. He has taught at Ohio University, Northern Illinois University (DeKalb), and at the State University of New York, College at Brockport, as well as in Turkey and The People's Republic of China.

Anchor Dragging, Anthony Piccione's first book-length collection of poems, was selected by Archibald MacLeish for BOA Editions, Ltd.'s New Poets of America Series in 1977. Chapbooks of his poetry include: *Nearing Land* (1975), *Is There Somewhere We Shouldn't Look?* (1978) and *Then It Was My Birthday* (1982).

Anthony Piccione and his family currently reside in Brockport, New York.